I0139824

STRICTLY ACADEMIC

A R Gurney

BROADWAY PLAY PUBLISHING INC
224 E 62nd St, NY, NY 10065
www.broadwayplaypub.com
info@broadwayplaypub.com

STRICTLY ACADEMIC
© Copyright 2008 by A R Gurney

All rights reserved. This work is fully protected under the copyright laws of the United States of America. No part of this publication may be photocopied, reproduced, stored in a retrieval system, or transmitted, in any form or by any means, electronic, mechanical, recording, or otherwise, without the prior permission of the publisher. Additional copies of this play are available from the publisher.

Written permission is required for live performance of any sort. This includes readings, cuttings, scenes, and excerpts. For amateur and stock performances, please contact Broadway Play Publishing Inc. For all other rights contact Peter Franklin, the William Morris Agency Inc, 1325 6th Ave, NY NY 10019.

First printing: December 2008
I S B N: 0-88145-248-3

Book design: Marie Donovan
Word processing: Microsoft Word
Typographic controls: Xerox Ventura Publisher 2.0 P E
Typeface: Palatino
Printed and bound in the U S A

CONTENTS

ABOUT THE AUTHOR

A R Gurney has written many plays. Among them are: THE DINING ROOM, THE COCKTAIL HOUR, LOVE LETTERS, SYLVIA, FAR EAST, and INDIAN BLOOD. He has also written several novels, a few television scripts, and the libretto of a one-act opera. He has received a number of awards including ones from the Drama Desk, the National Endowment of the Arts, the Rockefeller Foundation. He is a member of The American Academy of Arts and Letters, of the Theater Hall of Fame, and a Lucille Lortel Award winner for the body of his work. He has honorary degrees from Williams College and Buffalo State College S U N Y. He taught literature at M I T for many years before committing himself to full-time writing.

THE
PROBLEM

An earlier version of THE PROBLEM is published by Samuel French Inc, by whose permission this revised version is published.

The production of STRICTLY ACADEMIC opened at Primary Stages on 21 October 2003. The cast and creative contributors to THE PROBLEM were:

HUSBAND . . . . .Keith Reddin
WIFE . . . . Susan Greenhill

Director . . . . Paul Benedict
Set design . . . . .James Noone
Costume design . . . . .Laura Crow

CHARACTERS & SETTING

A HUSBAND, *a professor of mathematics at an urban university*
A WIFE, *an inner city social worker.*

Both are in early middle age.

The HUSBAND's study, indicated by a work table, a couple of chairs, and possibly a bookcase behind.

(At rise, the HUSBAND *hovers over a work table, creating geometrical figures with a V-shaped compass, a rule, and perhaps a small calculator. After a moment his* WIFE *comes in. She carries a briefcase and overcoat, and is obviously pregnant.)*

WIFE: Hey.

HUSBAND: *(Deep into drawing geometrical configurations)* I'm working, dear.

WIFE: I know, but look.

HUSBAND: I'm figuring out a very complicated proof in advanced geometry, dear.

WIFE: I know, but at least take a look. *(She moves closer to him and sticks out her stomach.)* Just a quick peek in my general direction.

*(*HUSBAND *turns his head and look right at her stomach. He starts, puts on glasses, takes another look.)*

HUSBAND: Well, well.

WIFE: You see?

HUSBAND: Surprise, surprise.

WIFE: Oh yes.

HUSBAND: Merry Christmas.

WIFE: Exactly.

HUSBAND: Why didn't I notice before?

WIFE: Because I wear rather loose-fitting clothes.

HUSBAND: That's true.

WIFE: Hip-length jackets. Extra large sweaters.

HUSBAND: True.

WIFE: Large, shapeless flannel nightgowns.

HUSBAND: True enough.

WIFE: So only now, tonight, is it beginning to show.

HUSBAND: Yes it shows. It definitely shows.... *(He looks at his watch.)* But I've got to work out this proof, dear. I meet my evening class in topological paradigms in less than an hour.

WIFE: Oh I know. And I've got a special meeting with my fellow social workers on various ethnic communities within the inner city.

HUSBAND: *(Returning to his work)* So we both should go about our business...I must say it's a great pleasure to turn from the computer to the more traditional tools of my trade.

WIFE: *(Indicating her stomach)* This is traditional, too.

HUSBAND: Good point, darling.

WIFE: I just thought you should know, that's all. So you could plan.

HUSBAND: I will. I'll plan accordingly.

(WIFE starts off, then stops.)

WIFE: One thing, though. One problem.

HUSBAND: *(As he works)* And what's that, dear.

WIFE: I don't know whether you've thought about this or not.

HUSBAND: State the problem. I'll tell you whether I've thought about it.

WIFE: It's a little tricky.

HUSBAND: Well then let's try to solve it together. We're married, after all.

WIFE: That's what makes it a little tricky.

HUSBAND: But that's also why you should feel comfortable speaking out.

WIFE: Good point. All right. You see, I'm not absolutely sure that this is yours.

(The HUSBAND *finishes a calculation at his work table, takes off his glasses, looks at her stomach again, and then looks up.)*

HUSBAND: Ah hah.

WIFE: You see?

HUSBAND: So that's the problem.

WIFE: That's the problem.

HUSBAND: I think I'll trust you on this one, dear.

WIFE: That's sweet of you, darling.... But can I trust myself?

HUSBAND: I think you should. So there we are.

WIFE: But...

HUSBAND: But what, dear?

WIFE: The thing is.... Now how do I put this?

HUSBAND: Speak frankly now.

WIFE: I'll try. The thing is...that you and I...haven't made love very much recently.

HUSBAND: Is that true?

WIFE: I think it is. Not very much. Not recently.

HUSBAND: Define "recently".

WIFE: Well, I mean...five years, more or less... give or take a month or two.

HUSBAND: My gosh, has it been that long?

WIFE: I believe so. Yes.

HUSBAND: And so you mind, obviously.

WIFE: Mind? Why should I mind?

HUSBAND: Well then I really don't see much of a problem. *(Starts to return to his work)*

WIFE: *(Pointing to her stomach)* I'm just thinking of this, that's all.

HUSBAND: Oh *that*.

WIFE: You see?

HUSBAND: Of course! Now I see the connection! *(Slaps his head.)* Dumb! Mr Dumb-bell here! Forgive me, darling. I was thinking about my class. I've been trying to devise a workable approximation for squaring the circle...

WIFE: Oh heavens, you certainly love your work, don't you? You're very involved in it.

HUSBAND: Yes I am, but I'm involved with *you* now. I'm very much on your wavelength.

WIFE: I knew you would be.

HUSBAND: So. Well. Now. What you seem to be saying is...stop me if I step out of line here...but what you're really saying is that you think someone else might have impregnated you.

WIFE: More or less. Yes.

HUSBAND: I see, I see, I see.

WIFE: It's possible, after all.

HUSBAND: Oh sure. It's a viable proposition.

WIFE: On these evenings when you go out to teach.

HUSBAND: Or when you go out to one of your evening meetings.

WIFE: Yes. All right. That, too. Yes.

HUSBAND: So we do have a problem there, don't we?

WIFE: Yes we do. We definitely do.

(*Pause.* HUSBAND *taps his teeth with his compass, scratches his head*)

HUSBAND: You know darling...it occurs to me...that I should have made love to you more.

WIFE: Oh no, no, no.

HUSBAND: I'm kicking myself now.

WIFE: Oh don't Please don't.

HUSBAND: I am. Things would now be much simpler.

WIFE: Oh sweetheart, stop punishing yourself.

HUSBAND: But why didn't I? Darn it. Darn it all.

WIFE: Darling, you have your work.

HUSBAND: Oh sure, but ...

WIFE: You have your equations and proofs and things.

HUSBAND: Sure I do, but darling, that doesn't really answer the question. The question remains why can't I do both? Why can't I both do advanced math and make love to you. Not at the same time, of course. But at least sequentially. Why haven't I done that? Why haven't I found the opportunity to make love to you in the past five years. That's the question that interests me at the moment.

WIFE: Well. I may have some sort of an answer.

HUSBAND: Tell me. Please.

WIFE: You used to laugh too much, maybe.

HUSBAND: Laugh?

WIFE: Yes. In the old days. Whenever we started to make love, you'd start to chuckle.

HUSBAND: *(Chuckling)* I did, didn't I? I remember now.

WIFE: Yes you would. You'd chuckle.

HUSBAND: Because the whole thing struck me as somewhat absurd... *(Chuckles)* And somewhat inelegant. *(Pause)* From a mathematical perspective. *(Chuckling)* I should have learned to control myself. *(Tries to, can't, bursts into loud laughter)* I'm sorry.

WIFE: Oh don't be sorry. I was just as bad.

HUSBAND: Did you chuckle too?

WIFE: No, actually, I'd cry.

HUSBAND: I don't remember your crying.

WIFE: Well I'd whimper.

HUSBAND: Yes, yes you would! You'd whimper. *(He chuckles.)*

WIFE: Well I felt so sad. Making love, while all these horrible things were going on in the larger world.

HUSBAND: So you'd whimper. Of course. It all comes back.

WIFE: Poverty and racism here at home. Injustice and political violence abroad. Terrorism everywhere.... It is all came surging in on me. I felt so guilty.

HUSBAND: And I felt so absurd.

WIFE: You chuckling, me whimpering.... It wasn't very conducive.

HUSBAND: Right. So we gave it up. So that answers that. *(Returns to his work)*

WIFE: But now...

HUSBAND: What?

WIFE: There's this. *(Indicates her stomach)*

HUSBAND: Oh right. *(As he works)* Keep it.

WIFE: What?

HUSBAND: Have it. Keep it. Bring it home.

WIFE: Oh darling...

HUSBAND: Give it my name. Consider me its father.
Remind me now and then to behave like one.

WIFE: Oh sweetheart...

HUSBAND: I've let you down. I'll make it up. So keep
the damn thing.

WIFE: But I'm partly to blame.

HUSBAND: But I'm the man.

WIFE: Oh yes you are! You certainly are the man!

HUSBAND: *(Indicating his work)* So now I've really got
to wrestle this problem to the ground.

WIFE: Of course. And I've got to get to my meeting.

*(They smile at each other. He returns to his work, she starts
out. Then she stop and stands thinking. After a moment he
looks up.)*

HUSBAND: But you're not satisfied.

WIFE: Oh I am, I am.

HUSBAND: Darling, we've been married over ten years.
I like to think I know you. And I think it's safe to say
you are definitely not satisfied.

WIFE: But you're in the middle of an important proof...

HUSBAND: My wife comes first. Come on. What's the
problem?

WIFE: I'm embarrassed even to bring it up.

HUSBAND: Come on. Out with it. Tell Daddy.

WIFE: All right... What if this... *(Indicates her stomach)* ...turns out to be black.

HUSBAND: Black?

WIFE: Depending on how the chromosomes line up.

HUSBAND: Black, eh?

WIFE: It's a possibility. I mean, can you still claim to be its father if it turns out to be black?

HUSBAND: Hmmm. *(Slyly)* That puts a different complexion on things.

WIFE: *(Giggling)* Oh you.

HUSBAND: *(Chuckling)* That's a horse of a different color.

WIFE: *(Laughing)* Now cut it out.... You're awful.... Try to be serious, please.

HUSBAND: *(Settling down)* O K, O K. Let's settle down here. Let's just settle down.

WIFE: I suppose I should have raised this issue before.

HUSBAND: No, no. I shouldn't have assumed....

WIFE: The problem of color just didn't occur to me.

HUSBAND: I'm very glad it didn't. That says something for America these days.

WIFE: But it may be a problem nonetheless. I mean personally. As far as we're concerned.

HUSBAND: It may be indeed. So now you must let me think it out.

WIFE: But you have your mathematics class. You have all those bright graduate students waiting for your words.

HUSBAND: I'll just be less prepared than I like to be. Which may be good. Which may be very good. Because mathematics is less cut and dried than one might think. It can be an enterprise based to some degree on intuition and improvisation. So I'll just have to wing it in class. I'll have to perform without a net underneath me. Which might be quite exciting, both for me and for my students.

WIFE: Oh I hope so, darling.

HUSBAND: But meanwhile, let me focus on our problem.

(He thinks. WIFE *stands watching him.)*

HUSBAND: Suppose I still claimed to be the child's father.

WIFE: How?

HUSBAND: We could tell the world that the hospital confused our child with a black one. Which we adopted. To avoid seeming racist.

WIFE: Sounds a little complicated.

HUSBAND: I know.

WIFE: A little baroque.

HUSBAND: I agree.

WIFE: Besides the natural father might object.

HUSBAND: Why?

WIFE: He might take pride in it himself.

HUSBAND: Need he know?

WIFE: I think it's only fair to tell him.

HUSBAND: I suppose. Yes.

WIFE: So he might want to see it.

HUSBAND: That seems natural enough.

WIFE: So he might want to come around.... After I'm home from the hospital....

HUSBAND: Well fine. .Let him.

WIFE: Yes, but also...

HUSBAND: Also? There's a corollary here?

WIFE: Well I mean he may want to resume sexual intercourse.

HUSBAND: You think?

WIFE: When I'm capable of it again.

HUSBAND: Yes. I see. Of course. Because you're a very attractive woman, darling.

WIFE: Thank you...

HUSBAND: I mean that. I don't blame the guy.

WIFE: But if he does come around, could you still adapt—I mean, adopt?

HUSBAND: Are you saying I might balk at the arrangement?

WIFE: Balk. That's the word. Balk.

HUSBAND: You know something, darling? I damn well might.

WIFE: You see? There you are. You're balking.

HUSBAND: I guess I am. So it's still a problem.

WIFE: But you want to get back to work....

HUSBAND: No, no, now wait a minute. *(He thinks carefully.)* I'm rethinking the problem. *(Thinks)* And I'm coming to a decision.... *(Comes to a conclusion)* O K. Fine. That's it.... Sweetheart, I'm going to be honest with you. *(Indicates chair)* Sit down, please.

WIFE: I can't sit down. Your feet are on that chair.

HUSBAND: You're right. I'll remove my feet so that you can sit.

WIFE: All right, I'll sit. Thank you, dear. *(She sits.)*

HUSBAND: Now don't look at me, darling. Face forward. Because this is going to be hard for me to tell, and harder still for you to hear.

WIFE: All right. I won't look at you.

HUSBAND: And if I seem vague or inarticulate about this, you must try to understand this is a difficult thing for a man to tell his wife. I'm only doing it—I'm only telling you—because it seems like the only way to solve this problem.

WIFE: Yes, yes. This problem.

HUSBAND: Now try not to interrupt, darling, unless you have to. Save your remarks and comments for the end. Unless you're unclear about some step in my argument. All right?

WIFE: I'll try.

HUSBAND: All right. *(Deep breath)* Now. To begin with, I've been lying to you this evening.

WIFE: Lying?

HUSBAND: Ssshh. Lying. I don't have a class tonight. I've never had a class at night. I don't believe in evening classes. By then, most students are too tired to do serious mathematics, and frankly so am I. So the class I've said meets at night actually meets on Mondays, Wednesdays, and Fridays at ten in the morning.

WIFE: I see.

HUSBAND: You may well ask, therefore, where I go on these nights when I say I have classes. And that is what so difficult to tell you. The fact is, I don't leave this building. Not really. Oh I leave by the front door, all right, but I immediately circle around to the service entrance and , since I already have a key, I reenter the edifice and go down to the cellar.

WIFE: The cellar.

HUSBAND: The cellar. Now what do I do in the cellar? You're probably asking yourself that. What do I do down there? ...Don't look at me, darling... Here's what I do in the cellar. I make my way to a small space behind the hot water heater. And there I have hidden...certain items. What have I hidden, you well may ask. So I'll tell you...I have hidden a tube of theatrical make-up. A wig. A complete change of clothes. And a mirror. That's what I have hidden in the cellar.

WIFE: I see.

HUSBAND: Yes. You see, love. Or you're beginning to. Now what I do is I set the mirror up on an adjacent water pipe. I strip to the buff. I daub my pallid skin from head to toe with a rich shade of burnished burnt umber. I glue on a race-appropriate wig. I don a color-coordinated ensemble of downtown garb. Then I leave the cellar. Reenter by the front door of the building. Take elevator up to this apartment. And ring for you. So you see, my poor darling, I am the dark stranger who has graced your bed, and have been all along.

WIFE: You.

HUSBAND: Me. Oh I know it sounds implausible. But remember how you like subdued lighting. Remember, too, that I played Othello in high school. For these reasons, I have somehow been able to deceive you for now these many years—disguising myself as member of a once-enslaved minority, and capitalizing on the sympathy you naturally feel for that gallant race.

WIFE: But...why did you do all this?

HUSBAND: Because I wanted to make love to you. And somehow this seemed like the best way to do it. You'll have to admit it worked.

WIFE: *(Looking at her stomach)* Oh yes. It worked.

HUSBAND: So out of all this subterfuge and depravity, at least a child will be born. And I am its father, after all.

WIFE: I have to say I'm somewhat taken aback by what you've told me.

HUSBAND: Of course you are. *(Gets up)* I hope you'll try to assimilate it while I'm gone.

WIFE: Gone?

HUSBAND: I'm going down to the cellar now.

WIFE: To put on your costume?

HUSBAND: No. To burn it.

WIFE: Burn it?

HUSBAND: Yes. It's all over now, my darling. The mask is off. Any attempt to wear it again would be foolish and self-conscious. Our love life would fast become as absurd as it was before I found this way to circumvent it. So I'm going to destroy my role. And when I come back, I want you gone.

WIFE: Gone?

HUSBAND: You must leave me now.

WIFE: I can't.

HUSBAND: You must. Oh my darling, this urge to love you is still in me. Who knows what oblique form it will take next. Take the child and go.

WIFE: Never.

HUSBAND: Please, darling. Oh listen. I don't know what I'll think of next, down in the cellar. I've got stacks of X-rated magazines down there. And a complete collection of the Marquis de Sade. I'll peruse them all, seeking out increasingly complicated arabesques of sexual perversion. I may reappear with a whip. Or wearing riding boots. Or dressed as a woman. Get out, darling. Run to the suburbs. Give my child a normal home. Go!

WIFE: Normal? Normal? What is normal?

HUSBAND: You are, my love, and thank heaven for it.

WIFE: Oh my God, how little do you know.... Sit down, please. I also have a tale to tell-o.

HUSBAND: Nothing you could say...

WIFE: Please sit down....

HUSBAND: Nothing...

WIFE: Listen: I've known all along you were my dusky lover.

HUSBAND: You've known?

WIFE: From the beginning.

HUSBAND: But how?

WIFE: Five years ago, when you announced that you had scheduled some evening classes, I became suspicious, knowing how you felt about teaching at that inconvenient hour. And so when you left for your class, I followed you.

HUSBAND: Followed me?

WIFE: Yes. Followed my own husband. Followed you to that tacky novelty store where you bought your theatrical disguises. Followed you back and into the cellar, where I hid behind the oil burner, and watched you change into your poor, pathetic imitation of an African-American.

HUSBAND: You spied on me.

WIFE: Yes, I spied on you, my darling. Furtively, suspiciously, like some aging matron seeking evidence for a divorce. But when I saw what you were doing, when I understood you were doing it for me, my heart went out to you. With a great rush of longing, I dashed back upstairs, eager to receive you but at the same time terrified that you'd see that I was onto your game. Frantically, I dimmed the lights to make things easier for both of us.

HUSBAND: I thought it was because you had become romantic.

WIFE: I know you did, darling, and I let you think that.

HUSBAND: You were acting? The whole time?

WIFE: Yes, wasn't I good? Pretending that you were someone new and strange? I, who am no actress, improvising like a professional during that whole scene.

HUSBAND: It's hard to believe. You seemed so...excited.

WIFE: I was. I was terribly excited. That strange, sly courtship, the unfamiliar street talk with those scintillating racial overtones—I was almost overwhelmed. But then when you carried me into the bedroom, everything changed.

HUSBAND: What do you mean? Wasn't I good?

WIFE: You were wonderful. But I wasn't.

HUSBAND: You said you loved me.

WIFE: I was only pretending. I really hated you.

HUSBAND: Hated me?

WIFE: And hated myself. It was horrible. I felt so guilty.

HUSBAND: Guilty?

WIFE: There was obviously a reverse kind of racism permeating the whole experience. I wanted at least to whimper, as I did normally with you, when you were white, but now that your pigmentation was more exotic, I began to wonder whether it was only your blackness which was turning me on. I found myself riddled with anxiety. I forced myself to pretend, to fake the most authentic experience a woman can have. And all the time I felt like a thing, an object, a creature without a soul, a poor, pathetic concubine in the arms of an Ethiopian potentate. And when you left—finally left—I just lay on the bed, my arms folded across my breast, like a stone carving gracing my own tomb. It took every ounce of energy I could muster to rise and greet you at the door when you returned somewhat later from your supposed class in higher mathematics.

HUSBAND: So for the past five years, you have been through hell.

WIFE: No.

HUSBAND: No?

WIFE: After that first ghastly evening, I suffered nothing.

HUSBAND: You mean, you were numbed by the experience?

WIFE: I mean I wasn't there.

HUSBAND: You weren't there?

WIFE: I left the apartment right after you went into the cellar.

HUSBAND: But then who...was here...with me?

WIFE: I got a substitute.

HUSBAND: A substitute.

WIFE: Oh darling, try to understand. I simply could not endure another evening like that. The sham, the pretense, the racial reversals—it all revolted me. And yet I knew how much the experience meant to you! All the next day, I racked my brain trying to figure out a solution to our problem. I took a long walk. I

wandered all over town. Finally, toward evening,
I happened to see a woman who looked a little like me.
Same hair, same height, roughly the same age. Could
she be the solution? I approached her and asked her
if she'd like to sleep with a member of a minority.
Naturally she said she would. So for the past five years,
this good woman has come here while you were in the
cellar changing your clothes, and in the dim light she
has pretended to be me.

HUSBAND: I see.

WIFE: Do you hate me very much?

HUSBAND: No, though I have to say I am somewhat
surprised.

WIFE: I suspected you would be.

HUSBAND: I suppose this is one of those things that
married couples must learn to live with.

WIFE: That's a positive way of looking at it.

HUSBAND: We get hit with the news, we wonder how
we can go on, and yet by God, we do.

WIFE: That's it.

HUSBAND: *(Pointing to her stomach)* Of course, there's
still that.

WIFE: Oh right. *(Holding her stomach)* This.

HUSBAND: Yes that. I still have to ask just whose is that?

WIFE: Now bear with me, darling. On those nights
when you're in the cellar and while this good woman
waits at the apartment for your return, I go off with
a gentleman from Cameroon.

HUSBAND: Cameroon?

WIFE: Or Liberia, I forget which. He rings the bell and
off we go to that section of the city which is populated

primarily by immigrants from West Africa. There, to the tune of some of the most exciting rhythms since the early George Gershwin, we make love—love which for the first time in my life I can give myself up to, since with him I feel that I am expiating not only my own guilt but the guilt of all America for its long neglect of the dark continent.

HUSBAND: Darling, I'm somewhat concerned—

WIFE: Stop right there. I assure you that I was firmly committed to protected sex, and so were my partners.

HUSBAND: "Partners", darling? You used the plural?

WIFE: Somehow my relationship with the West African gentleman wasn't enough. I felt there was more to do. So I betrayed my lover for his friend from Somalia. And him for a gentleman from Turkey. And soon I was involved with various representatives from the Asian subcontinent and Latin America, along with several men from the northern temperate zones. Oh darling, for the last five years I have been sleeping with legal and illegal immigrants, from all over the world.

HUSBAND: And so the father of your child is...

WIFE: America's global responsibilities, and my attempt to give them a human face.

HUSBAND: Oh boy.

WIFE: And now you'll leave me, won't you?

HUSBAND: Leave you?

WIFE: To bear my child alone while off you go.

HUSBAND: Me? Go now? *(He laughs peculiarly.)* I want to stay more than ever. *(He returns to his geometrical problem, drawing another careful circle with his compass.)* What would you say...if I said...that everything you've told me...excites me?

WIFE: Excites you?

HUSBAND: Sets my blood boiling. Gives me strange, wild frissons of desire. What would you say if I said that your experiences with alternate cultures have lit a lurid light in my own loins?

WIFE: Really?

HUSBAND: *(Still working on his geometrical problem)* What would you say...if I said...that I want to exercise—how shall I put it? —*mon droit de seigneur* on you? That I want to steal you from the peasants, so to speak, and carry you to the bedroom, and ravage you with our reading lights going full blaze?

WIFE: I'd say...do it.

HUSBAND: Bravo!

WIFE: And let me add this. Looking at you now, brooding over your work-table, obsessed with abstract signs and peculiar shapes, I suddenly have the strange desire to experience the stale comforts of localized married love. They say that Americans in Paris, surfeited by the rich food, yearn for bland delights of McDonald's hamburgers. So it is with me. For you. Tonight.

HUSBAND: *(Turning from his work)* Then...

WIFE: But there's still this. *(Indicating her stomach)* This problem.

HUSBAND: *(Holding his compass, moving toward her)* That's no problem.

WIFE: No problem?

HUSBAND: That's just the premise to the problem. Now that we've solved the problem, we no longer need the premise.

WIFE: I fail to follow.

HUSBAND: That's just the starting mechanism. Now the motor's going. we no longer need the starter.

WIFE: *(Looking at her stomach)* I'm still somewhat confused.

HUSBAND: That's not really a baby you have in there.

WIFE: *(Backing away)* Not really a baby?

HUSBAND: That's a balloon you have in there.

WIFE: Oh now...

HUSBAND: A balloon. Or a bladder. Or an old beach ball.

WIFE: It's a baby. I'm practically positive.

HUSBAND: No, no. Look. I'll demonstrate the proof.... *(He takes his compass, assumes a fencing stance, and gives her a quick, neat jab with its sharp point.)* Touche! *(There's a pop, a hissing sound asnd then she slowly deflates.)* You see? The problem was strictly academic.

(Pause)

WIFE: Aren't we awful?

HUSBAND: You started it.

WIFE: It was my turn. You started the last one.

HUSBAND: Well it's fun. *(He looks at her and gives a long Tarzan-like whoop, then pounds his chest.)* Ssshhh! Quiet! You'll wake the children!

(HUSBAND picks her up in his arms. She pummels him melodramatically, speaks with an English accent)

HUSBAND: No, Tarzan! No! White men do not take women by force! They court their women, Tarzan! It's very complicated . Do you understand what I'm saying? Com-pli-ca-ted...C-O-M.... *(He carries her manfully offstage.)*

END OF PLAY

THE
GUEST
LECTURER

THE GUEST LECTURER was first performed on
24 October 1998 at the George Street Playhouse in
New Brunswick, New Jersey (David Saint, Artistic
Director; Tom Werder, Managing Director). The cast
and creative contributors were:

PAT .... Mary Ehlinger
MONA ....Nancy Opel
HARTLEY .... Robert Stanton
FRED .... Rex Robbins

Director .... John Rando
Set design ....Rob Odorisio
Costume design ....David Murin
Lighting design .... Dan Kotlowitz
Music composition .... Tom Cabaniss
Stage manager ....K R Williams

As a companion piece to THE PROBLEM, with the
same administrative and creative staffs, THE GUEST
LECTURER also opened at Primary Stages on
21 October 2003 with the following cast:

PAT .... Amy Southerland
MONA .... Susan Greenhill
HARTLEY ....Remy Auberjonois
FRED ....Keith Reddin

Original music .... Tom Cabaniss
Lyrics ....A R Gurney

THE GUEST LECTURER should be staged as simply and straightforwardly as possible. Any attempt to theatricalize them by adding fanciful stage effects, shifts in lighting, or extra sound cues will do more harm than good. The overriding form of THE GUEST LECTURER should first, last, and always be that of a simple lecture-discussion held on the stage of a regional or community theater.

CHARACTERS & SETTING

MONA
HARTLEY
FRED
PAT, *a piano player, who may be either male or female*

Upstage, a curtain extending the width of the stage. In front of it, on either side, an American flag balanced by another flag of local significance. Downstage center, two chairs with a low table between them. On the table, a silver tray holding a silver water pitcher and a pair of silver goblets. Also on the table, a small vase containing a single flower. Downstage right, an upright piano.

(PAT *enters, plays an overture of lively show tunes.*
She seems as surprised by her talent as we are.
When she finishes, MONA *enters anxiously.)*

MONA: *(Hurriedly)* Thank you, Pat... *(Coming down
to audience)* For those who are new here, I'm Mona
Hammersmith, the Artistic Director of this theater.
(Holding up her hands) Please don't applaud. We
don't have time. *(Glancing off left)* Our guest lecturer
is finishing his dinner next door. Fred Sadler, the
President of our Board is with him, and will bring
him over as soon as they've had their decaf
cappuccinos. Bruce, our stage manager, will signal us
when they arrive... *(Waving toward off left)* Right, Bruce?
(Comes closer to audience) Now, I have a confession to
make. I was the one who ordered those cappuccinos.
Why? So I could duck out and speak to you... Now,
how do I say this? ...Lately I've been wondering if
our guest lecture series is getting a little out of hand.
I mean, are we really doing the right thing, inviting
people here, and then...I don't know. I'm beginning
to have serious reservations.

(Chord from PAT*)*

MONA: Did Bruce signal, Pat? Are they here?

(PAT *nods.)*

MONA: They are here. *(Quickly; confidingly to audience)*
I just wish we could find a better way of doing things,
that's all. *(To* PAT*)* Hit it, Pat.

(PAT *plays a fanfare.)*

MONA: *(To audience)* Now you can applaud. Because here comes our Chairman of the Board.

(She leads applause. FRED *comes on. He is middle-aged and wears a business suit.)*

FRED: *(To audience)* Ladies and gentlemen, our guest lecturer.

*(*PAT *plays another fanfare.)*

MONA: *(To audience)* Now you can applaud some more.

*(*MONA *and* FRED *encourage applause.* HARTLEY *comes out. He is young and academic-looking, dressed in khakis, jacket and tie. He blinks in the light.)*

HARTLEY: *(To audience)* Thank you. Thank you so much...

FRED: *(Thumbing through a number of pages)* Hartley Carr comes to us from... *(Finds it)*...the Graduate Program in Dramatic Arts at the University of Southern Ohio.

HARTLEY: That's right.

FRED: He will speak to us tonight on.... *(Finding it again)* Drama in America.

*(*PAT *plays a snatch of the national anthem.)*

HARTLEY: That's it.

MONA: *(To audience)* Hartley is our first lecturer to speak specifically about the theater. And he's unusual in another way. Normally we write to various universities and ask for a guest lecturer. This year Hartley wrote to *us*.

HARTLEY: I did.

MONA: You might tell us why, Hartley.

HARTLEY: Well. *(He moves awkwardly into centerstage.)* I'm writing my thesis on the future of American drama. I believe it lies in the regional theater movement. I read somewhere that your group is doing particularly well, so I wanted to check you out.

FRED: *(To audience)* Hear that, folks? We're the future of American drama!

(He encourages applause. PAT plays another fanfare.)

MONA: I hope we can help you, Hartley.

HARTLEY: And I hope I can help *you*—by pinpointing what you're doing right.

MONA: Oh, I'm sure there are things we're doing wrong.

FRED: What do you mean by that, Mona?

MONA: Oh, nothing.

FRED: Are you having second thoughts?

MONA: Oh, no, no, no.

FRED: You are. *(To audience)* She's getting cold feet. I can tell.

MONA: *(To audience)* Oh, maybe just a little.

FRED: Don't.

MONA: I'll try not to.

FRED: If it ain't broke, don't fix it. O K?

MONA: O K, O K.

FRED: Just keep your eye on the goddam ball! *(Turning to HARTLEY)* Well. I'll get offstage. Have fun, fella. *(Claps him on the back)*

HARTLEY: Thanks.

FRED: *(To MONA, threateningly)* I'll be watching, kiddo. *(He goes.)*

(Pause)

HARTLEY: *(To MONA)* What was that all about?

MONA: Oh, nothing. *(Indicating pianist)* Please. Meet Pat.

HARTLEY: *(Crossing, shaking hands)* Hi, Pat.

(PAT *plays a bar or two of* Hail, Hail, the Gang's All Here.)

HARTLEY: I didn't know I'd get a piano.

MONA: Oh, tonight you get lots of things.... So let's get started. *(Indicating the chairs and table)* As I told you before, we use a discussion format for our Guest Lecturer series. No lecterns or microphones. We just sit and talk.

HARTLEY: Fine by me.

MONA: *(Indicating the stage right chair)* You get what we call "the danger seat"....

(PAT *plays creepy danger music.*)

HARTLEY: The danger seat?

MONA: Just an expression that seems to have caught on over the years... *(Indicating the chair on the left)* Whereas I occupy what's know as "the driver's seat".

HARTLEY: The driver's seat...

MONA: Because I drive things along.

(PAT *plays a little of the overture to* William Tell.)

MONA: I'm the facilitator.

HARTLEY: The facilitator.

MONA: So let me facilitate you into that chair.

HARTLEY: Sure. Fine.

(They sit.)

MONA: And of course it's first names out here, by the way. I'll call you Hartley, and you call me Mona.

HARTLEY: All right, Mona.

MONA: You do the talking, and I'll ask questions or make comments.

HARTLEY: Fine.

MONA: And there will be occasional underscoring by Pat.

(PAT *plays creepy suspense music.*)

HARTLEY: Why?

MONA: We've found over the years it leavens the lump.

HARTLEY: Oh.

MONA: And if you want to get up and move around, feel free to do so.

HARTLEY: May I?

MONA: Absolutely. We encourage it. It keeps people awake.

HARTLEY: Sometimes I do like to speak on my feet.

MONA: Oh, I hope you'll speak on more than just that.

(PAT *plays a vaudeville finish to a joke.*)

HARTLEY: What?

MONA: Just a dumb joke. I apologize. The point is, you're free to move. And so am I.

HARTLEY: You'll get up, too?

MONA: Oh, I used to just sit here with my legs crossed like a good little girl, but lately I've found that if I don't get up, I want to close my eyes and scream!

HARTLEY: I hope you won't do that.

MONA: I'll try not to. But if you're in the middle of making some important point, and I suddenly start pacing back and forth like a caged animal, at least you'll be prepared.

HARTLEY: I'm glad you told me. *(Pause)* Anything else?

MONA: Not for now. Anything from you, Pat?

(PAT *thinks, shakes her head.*)

MONA: Then why don't you start lecturing, Hartley?

HARTLEY: O K. *(Takes a stack of cards out of his breast pocket, speaks to audience)* First I want to thank you for responding to my request and inviting me here. I particularly want to thank *you*, Mona.

MONA: *(To audience)* I always meet our guest lecturers at the airport and take them home so they can freshen up.

HARTLEY: It was very thoughtful.

MONA: *(To audience)* I give them the guest room.

HARTLEY: And a nice room it is.

MONA: *(To audience)* It has its own bath.

HARTLEY: I thank you for your hospitality, Mona.

MONA: You're most welcome.

HARTLEY: *(To audience)* I also want to thank you good people for coming here this evening. I must say I'm impressed.

MONA: Impressed? Why?

HARTLEY: Do you always get this large a turnout?

MONA: More and more every year.

HARTLEY: Just for a guest lecturer?

MONA: Especially for a guest lecturer.

HARTLEY: That's unusual.

MONA: Of course, it may have something to do with... something to do with....

HARTLEY: Something to do with what?

MONA: Something to do with the... *(Under her breath)*
...the murder.

HARTLEY: I didn't hear you, Mona.

MONA: The murder.

HARTLEY: The murder?

MONA: We had a murder here.

HARTLEY: When?

MONA: Oh, awhile back.

HARTLEY: Who was killed?

MONA: I don't want to get into it, Hartley.

HARTLEY: But why would a murder make people want
to come to a lecture?

MONA: So we can be together.

HARTLEY: Ah.

MONA: To share our common concern.

HARTLEY: I see. You mean you need to reassert
your communal identity in the face of an ultimately
noncommunal act.

MONA: I guess that's it.

HARTLEY: *(To audience)* O K. Then let me say this.
I don't know who was killed around here. Or why.
But I'm sorry.

MONA: That's sweet, Hartley. Now let's move on.

HARTLEY: *(Checking his notes)* Maybe we should talk
about why people go to the theater.

MONA: Wait!

HARTLEY: What?

MONA: *(To audience)* I forgot to mention the water. Maybe I've been doing this too long. *(Indicating the pitcher)* There's water here, Hartley.

HARTLEY: I see that.

MONA: Good, cool ice water... This town of ours may be totally polluted in other ways, but our drinking water remains relatively pure. I think everyone in this room would agree on that.

HARTLEY: That's good to know.

MONA: Want some?

HARTLEY: No, thanks.

MONA: I can easily pour you some.

HARTLEY: Maybe later. O K?

MONA: Fair enough. *(She drinks.)*

HARTLEY: *(Checks his notes)* Let's talk about why people go to the theater.

MONA: Why wouldn't they?

HARTLEY: Well, I mean, lots of people don't, these days.

MONA: *We* go.

HARTLEY: I know. But you could have stayed home and watched T V....

MONA: Oh, that.

HARTLEY: Or gone to the movies. Or some athletic event.

MONA: Yawn, yawn.

HARTLEY: Or fooled around on the Internet. Or picked up a book...

MONA: A book? What's that?

HARTLEY: But instead of doing any of those things, you came here. Just to hear some guest lecturer. *(He gets up.)*

MONA: *(To audience)* He's getting up.

HARTLEY: Yes, I am, Mona. I'm getting up because I'm excited by the fact that a decent number of disparate people have coughed up hard-earned cash just to cluster together in tight rows of uncomfortable seats and hear some guest lecturer talk about that strange, occasionally thrilling, more often disappointing enterprise we call theater!

MONA: Well said.

HARTLEY: Now, why, I ask? Why have men and women gathered together over the years, over the centuries, by the flickering fire of some ancient druid's circle, or under the azure skies of classical Greece. *(To audience)* Or you, here, tonight. *(To MONA)* Why do we go, Mona?

MONA: You tell me.

HARTLEY: We go to the theater because we all believe, or want to believe, no, wrong, *need* to believe, that there is something profoundly fulfilling about the live— repeat *live*—transaction between the individual and the community.

MONA: That's beautifully said, Hartley. *(To audience)* See? Now here is a man who just gave us a complete summary of world drama without once mentioning murder.

HARTLEY: I'm still thinking about it, though. We all should.

MONA: Why? Why do we have to?

HARTLEY: Because it leads to the subject of communal guilt.

MONA: Oh, dear.

HARTLEY: I wish you could tell me more about it.

MONA: *(To audience)* He won't let it go, will he? He's like a dog with a bone.

HARTLEY: I just feel it may be relevant, that's all.

MONA: Oh, all right, then. What do you want to know?

HARTLEY: Has the murderer been brought to trial?

MONA: No.

HARTLEY: No?

MONA: No.

HARTLEY: Why not?

MONA: Again, it's very complicated.

HARTLEY: Do you mean the killer is still running around free?

MONA: I really think we should move on, Hartley. Otherwise we could get into very hot water.

HARTLEY: All right. *(To audience)* I just hope the killer is brought swiftly to justice, that's all. So that the community can reconstitute itself on healthier terms.

MONA: Thank you, Hartley. Now, for God's sake let's change the subject.

HARTLEY: *(Looking at his notes)* I'm sorry. This murder thing has thrown me all off.

MONA: Maybe a glass of water would help.

HARTLEY: No, thanks.

MONA: Mind if I pour myself one?

HARTLEY: Not at all.

MONA: You're sure it won't distract you?

HARTLEY: I said no!

MONA: Well, gee whiz! Don't get disagreeable!

HARTLEY: I'm sorry.

MONA: All I want is a simple glass of water. *(She pours herself a glass, drinks it, puts the glass back.)* There. Boy. Did I need that. *(She looks at HARTLEY.)* Now. Ready. Set. Go.

HARTLEY: All right. *(Pause)* I have to say one more thing about that murder.

MONA: Oh, Lord.

HARTLEY: *(To audience)* Even during the final throes of the Peloponnesian War, when the Spartan infantry was at the very gates of Athens, Athenian citizens, whose very lives were on the line, still found the time and the means to put on plays, and derived—

MONA: Excuse me, Hartley.

HARTLEY: What?

MONA: *(Indicating the audience)* They're getting bored.

HARTLEY: You think?

MONA: I know. I saw several people glancing at their watches.

HARTLEY: I'm sorry.

MONA: I think people want us to talk about sex.

HARTLEY: Sex?

MONA: It always perks things up.

HARTLEY: They want us to talk about sex in world drama?

MONA: No. Sex between you and me.

HARTLEY: What?

MONA: *(Indicating audience)* They're wondering if we've had sex. *(To audience)* And the answer to that is, yes, we have.

HARTLEY: Mona!

MONA: *(To audience)* We had sex this afternoon.
In the guest room.

HARTLEY: *(Whispering)* For Chrissake, Mona!

MONA: *(Whispering)* Don't swear, please. It offends
people.

HARTLEY: *(Whispering)* But it's none of their business!

MONA: *(Whispering)* Are you ashamed?

HARTLEY: *(Whispering)* No, I'm not ashamed.

MONA: *(Louder)* You are obviously ashamed of what
we did.

HARTLEY: *(Louder)* I am not ashamed, Mona!

MONA: *(To audience)* I myself feel no shame at all.
It was a spontaneous and life-affirming experience.
(To HARTLEY*)* And if I share my enthusiasm with
others, what's wrong with that? People should
know who you are.

HARTLEY: Who I am? Who I *am*? I'll tell you who I am.
(To audience) I'm a guy who arrives in a strange town
after a long flight and is greeted at the airport by a
strange woman....

MONA: Strange? Strange?

HARTLEY: Who takes me home and offers me her guest
room, and when I step out of the shower, guess who's
standing there waiting.

MONA: I was bringing you a clean towel!

HARTLEY: You were stark naked.

MONA: So were you! So were you stark naked!

HARTLEY: I was *supposed* to be!

MONA: Yes, well, I notice you rose to the occasion.

HARTLEY: I thought it was the polite thing to do.

MONA: Now, that's mean! That is a mean, ungenerous thing to say!

HARTLEY: Yes, well, you want people to know who I am. *(To audience)* So here's who I am, folks. I'm a guy who does not appreciate being publicaly humiliated in front of a bunch of strangers. That's who I am. All right? *(He walks off left.)*

MONA: *(Pause; to audience)* Oh, dear. Why do they always take it so seriously? Is it a male thing, or what? *(Calls off)* You signed a contract, sir! *(To audience)* He's sulking around in the wings. *(Calling off)* We are waiting, Hartley! *(To audience)* Oh, hell. Maybe we should just let him go—before it's too late. I'm serious. Maybe we should give this one a break. Except, if he goes, I'd never see him again.

(PAT plays a musical intro.)

MONA: Time for the song, Pat?

(PAT nods; MONA turns to the audience.)

MONA: Time for the song.

(PAT plays; MONA sings)

MONA: What's happening here?
What is the bidding?
Should I be showing my hand?...

(HARTLEY comes slowly back on stage; PAT stops playing.)

(Pause)

MONA: I'm glad you've reconsidered.

HARTLEY: The stage manager wouldn't let me leave.

MONA: That's Bruce. He takes his job very seriously.

HARTLEY: Yes, well, there are no planes out tonight anyway. It seems I'm trapped in this town.

MONA: Oh, don't put it that way.

HARTLEY: Yes, well, it feels that way.

MONA: Did you hear our song?

HARTLEY: Some of it.

MONA: I wrote it with Pat. *(Whispers)* Tell her you liked it.

HARTLEY: I'm not going—.

MONA: Tell her, for God's sake. She worked hard on it.

HARTLEY: I liked the song, Pat.

(PAT sulks a little.)

MONA: I'm glad you decided to come back, Hartley.

HARTLEY: Oh, hell. I guess if a President of the United States can give a major speech to Congress after he's been accused of gross sexual improprieties, I suppose a guest lecturer can give a talk about the theater after a consensual tryst with his facilitator.

MONA: *(Applauding)* There you go. *(To audience)* Isn't he adorable? See why I can't let him go?

HARTLEY: *(Looking at his notes)* I'm not sure where to pick up the thread.

MONA: *(Picking up the pitcher)* I don't know about you, but I'm having some more water.

HARTLEY: I'm not.

MONA: I hate to drink alone.

HARTLEY: *(With a sigh)* O K, I'll have a glass of water.

MONA: Good. *(She pours one for him.)* When two people share an activity it brings them together.

HARTLEY: Thanks. *(He sits, takes a sip absent-mindedly as he works through his notes; then he takes another sip; then he looks at his glass.)* This isn't water.

MONA: Isn't it?

HARTLEY: This is.... *(Taking another taste)* Vodka!

MONA: Is it?

HARTLEY: *(To audience)* This is almost straight vodka!

MONA: Actually it is.

HARTLEY: You said it was water.

MONA: I lied.

HARTLEY: Why did you lie?

MONA: Because I don't like announcing there's vodka in the water pitcher.

HARTLEY: But why *put* vodka in the water pitcher?

MONA: Because, Hartley, it might look a little cheap if we just brought out the bottle.

HARTLEY: No, but why vodka in the first place?

MONA: Because it looks like water.

HARTLEY: But why *serve* it, Mona?

MONA: Why does anyone serve alcohol? To loosen people up. To make things easier for all concerned.

HARTLEY: I know, but...

MONA: And is that so horrible? Is that the worst thing in the world? To try to make our guest lecturers feel a little more comfortable before they...before they....

HARTLEY: Before they what, Mona?

MONA: Before they go.

HARTLEY: Oh.

MONA: I'm sorry. I'm getting a little choked up here, all of a sudden.

HARTLEY: Mona...

MONA: I don't see why these evenings can't be fun? I don't see why these lectures have to be such a solemn, serious occasion? I happen to have worked very hard over the years to keep things going around here, and it seems to me you're fighting me tooth and nail. *(She starts to cry.)*

HARTLEY: *(To audience)* Oh, boy. *(To* MONA*)* Oh, Mona, Mona, Mona. *(He reaches across to her, pats her knee, offers her a handkerchief.)* Here. Use this.

MONA: *(Through her tears)* I'm sorry. I'm feeling a little torn lately. As Big Bad Fred out there will be only too glad to testify.

HARTLEY: Torn about what?

MONA: Never mind... I suppose you think I'm a lousy facilitator.

HARTLEY: No, no, no. I don't, Mona. *(To audience)* I really don't. *(He goes to her.)*

MONA: *(Putting his hand on her breast)* Here you are, seriously interested in the future of the American theater, and all I do is sleep with you and spike your drink.

HARTLEY: It's all *right*, Mona. No problem. No problem at all. Really. *(He takes a sip.)* Look, I'm drinking the vodka, Mona. I like it. See? I love it, Mona. It's my favorite thing. Look.

*(*MONA *watches him; he takes a big slug of it.)*

HARTLEY: Yummy. Great vodka.

MONA: *(Drying her eyes)* Thank you.

HARTLEY: You know what I think the real problem is?

MONA: What?

HARTLEY: The murder thing. It seems to brood over the evening.

MONA: You may be right.

HARTLEY: I'd really like to know more about it, Mona. It might affect my remarks on drama in America.

MONA: Yes. All right. I'll tell you. *(To audience)* Hold on to your hats, people. *(To HARTLEY)* Ask away. Ask anything you want, and I'll try to respond as clearly as I can.

HARTLEY: O K. *(Pause)* So somebody was killed around here.

MONA: Somebody was.

HARTLEY: A man or a woman?

MONA: A man, Hartley. Very much a man.

HARTLEY: Was he a leading citizen in this community?

MONA: Yes and no.

HARTLEY: Which means?

MONA: Which means that yes, he was a leading citizen, but no, he was not a member of this community.

HARTLEY: He was an outsider?

MONA: He was definitely an outsider.

HARTLEY: What was he doing here?

MONA: He was a guest lecturer.

(Pause)

HARTLEY: A guest...

MONA: Lecturer.

(Pause)

HARTLEY: He came here to give a talk and was killed?

MONA: Exactly.

HARTLEY: Why?

MONA: I don't know.

HARTLEY: Was it because of his lecture?

MONA: What do you mean?

HARTLEY: Was the subject of his lecture controversial?

MONA: No. Not really. No.

HARTLEY: Then it was a random killing?

MONA: Random?

HARTLEY: Was he the victim of a mugging?
Or some drive-by shooting?

MONA: Oh, no. It was planned.

HARTLEY: The murder was premeditated?

MONA: Thoroughly premeditated. And carefully
executed.

HARTLEY: How do you know?

MONA: From the way he was killed.

HARTLEY: Could you elaborate on that?

MONA: It's a little...raw.

HARTLEY: You said I should ask whatever I wanted.

MONA: All right, all right. *(Pause)* He was ritually
sacrificed.

HARTLEY: Ritually...?

MONA: Sacrificed.

HARTLEY: How?

MONA: You want to know the gory details?

HARTLEY: I do, Mona.

MONA: O K. *(She takes a deep breath.)* He was stripped
naked, castrated, and then strangled.

HARTLEY: Good God!

MONA: Or rather garroted.

HARTLEY: Garroted?

MONA: With a silken cord.

HARTLEY: A silken cord?

MONA: Or cotton. Whatever. The point is, the murder weapon was made from natural fibers.

HARTLEY: Wow!

MONA: You asked.

HARTLEY: I sure did. Boy. When did this happen?

MONA: Awhile back.

HARTLEY: When?

MONA: I don't remember the exact *date*, Hartley.

HARTLEY: But you are telling me that you had a guest lecturer who was ritually murdered and mutilated in the not-too-distant past.

MONA: That's exactly what I'm telling you.

HARTLEY: Is there anything else?

MONA: Anything *else*? Isn't that *enough*?

HARTLEY: I mean, are there any other circumstances that might shed light on the killing?

MONA: Oh. Oh, yes.

HARTLEY: Tell me.

MONA: I'll try. My tale begins soon after the war.

(She nods to PAT; PAT *plays a World War I song.)*

HARTLEY: Which war?

MONA: World War Two, actually.

*(*PAT *plays a World War II song.)*

MONA: Though I admit there have been too many others in this bleak segment of history we call the twentieth century.

HARTLEY: Go on, Mona.

MONA: After World War Two, my grandmother took it upon herself to establish a small community theater in this town.

HARTLEY: Your grandmother.

MONA: She felt that democracy and the theater went hand in hand. Democracy had won the war. So she wanted to celebrate the peace with three typically American plays.

HARTLEY: What did she select?

MONA: *They Knew What They Wanted, I Can Get It For You Wholesale,* and *You Can't Take It With You.*

HARTLEY: Sounds like a balanced program.

MONA: It was. And it attracted a sizeable audience. So much so, in fact, that she went professional, importing New York actors and presenting a wide range of works.

(PAT *plays quietly:* Give My Regards to Broadway.*)*

HARTLEY: Good for your grandmother.

MONA: But after a while, the operation began to lose steam. Audiences showed up dutifully, but there was something missing in their response. The sense of community was no longer there.

HARTLEY: Ah, well, you must remember, Mona, that good theater is a precarious flower. I salute your grandmother for trying to cultivate it.

MONA: My mother tried to keep things going.

(PAT*'s playing gets slower and sadder.)*

HARTLEY: Your mother? I sense a matriarchal theme emerging here.

MONA: She put on smaller and less expensive productions—things like *The Gin Game* and *Oleanna*—but something was still missing in the audience response.

HARTLEY: Did your mother try musicals? Did she reach out towards minorities?

MONA: Oh, yes. She put on an African-American version of *The Sound of Music.*

HARTLEY: And still the same flat response?

MONA: Very much so. The audience remained detached. Men yawned and looked at their watches. And women sighed and looked at their men.

HARTLEY: What you're describing is a general trend in American theater, Mona.

MONA: In all theater everywhere, Hartley. It killed my mother.

HARTLEY: Killed her?

MONA: She died of disappointment on a pilgrimage to London's West End. She hoped salvation lay in the English theater. But all she found was good accents and bad teeth.

HARTLEY: I'm sorry.

MONA: After my mother's death, I took over. I thought stars might be the solution. Or at least celebrities.

(PAT *plays a contemporary show tune.*)

MONA: But of course none of them would come. O K, then, I said. We'll create our *own* celebrities, at least for the evening. So in a final, frantic effort to fan the embers, I introduced our Guest Lecture Series.

(PAT *stops playing.*)

HARTLEY: You settled for simply lectures?

MONA: I thought lectures would at least bring people together and keep my grandmother's dream alive.

HARTLEY: Let me just say, Mona, that you have just given a capsule history of American drama—only in reverse. The lecture was very popular in the nineteenth century. Gradually it gave way to community and regional theater.

MONA: Interesting, if true. In any case, I began my lecture series by inviting a graduate student in political science to speak to us on the democratic experience. Our young scholar arrived. And spoke. To a small cluster of loyal, but disgruntled, subscribers.

HARTLEY: Did he speak well?

MONA: Not particularly. But something strange happened. Maybe the audience felt some profound yearning to move beyond politics, or maybe simply a need to connect, but something electric happened to the house that night. You could feel it almost from the start.

HARTLEY: There's nothing like a good evening in the theater!

MONA: Absolutely. But when I arrived backstage to congratulate the speaker and escort him to a small reception at a nearby Holiday Inn, I found him sprawled on a couch in the greenroom— naked, castrated, and garroted with a silken cord.

HARTLEY: How horrible!

MONA: It was not a pleasant sight, I can tell you.

HARTLEY: What crossed your mind, seeing that?

MONA: At first I thought he might have offended the political sensibilities of some of our subscribers....

HARTLEY: But that turned out not to be true?

MONA: I don't think so. I called the Young Republican Club the next day, and they denied all responsibility.

HARTLEY: I assume you also called the police.

MONA: Oh, yes. Immediately. But there wasn't much they could do.

HARTLEY: Why not?

MONA: They couldn't find the body.

HARTLEY: I thought you just said...

MONA: When I returned to the greenroom from the backstage payphone after dialing 9-1-1, the body had totally disappeared. I asked around, of course. But no one could provide a plausible explanation.

HARTLEY: Strange...

MONA: It was only later that several of our subscribers finally allowed as how it might have been consumed.

HARTLEY: Consumed?

MONA: At the reception at the Holiday Inn.

HARTLEY: Do you mean...?

MONA: Say it.

HARTLEY: Cannibalized?

MONA: That's it.

HARTLEY: Good gravy! This is a grim tale you've told, Mona.

MONA: You can see why I shied away from telling it.

HARTLEY: Your audience was obviously starved for drama.

MONA: Exactly. And that night they ate it up.

HARTLEY: Yes...

MONA: Are you shocked?

HARTLEY: In a way, no. What you've told me simply illustrates the basic undercurrent of violence that lies at the heart of America.

MONA: I suppose you're right.

HARTLEY: In fact, you could take it one step further. Read Freud's "Civilization and Its Discontents." Under the thin veneer of all civilized life lies a festering stew of chaos and disorder.

MONA: Oh, yes! Oh, yes!

HARTLEY: Which makes civilization all the more valuable. And good theater all the more important.

MONA: Absolutely!

HARTLEY: There's something else in your story which jogs my memory, Mona. I find myself mentally surfing through my files....

MONA: *(Pouring another drink)* While you're doing that, I hope you'll excuse me if I have a quick belt.

HARTLEY: I don't blame you. *(He thinks.)*

MONA: Maybe Pat will have one, too.

(PAT takes a glass out of her purse, puts it on the piano. MONA pours her a drink out of her goblet. PAT takes a can of peanuts out of her purse, puts it on the piano. MONA eats one.)

HARTLEY: *(Jumping up)* I've got it! What you've told me reminds me of something I learned when I was merely an undergraduate.

MONA: Tell me.

HARTLEY: First, I have to ask one more question.

MONA: Go ahead.

HARTLEY: This might be a little embarrassing to you.

MONA: Never mind. I can take it.

HARTLEY: O K. Here goes. Did you sleep with the murdered man? Before he was murdered, I mean.

MONA: Yes, I did.

HARTLEY: Knew it!

MONA: Are you jealous?

HARTLEY: Not at all!

MONA: Why not?

HARTLEY: Because it proves my point!

MONA: Explain that, please.

HARTLEY: Now, listen carefully: Remember when I said that, by retreating to the lecture form, you had returned to the roots of American drama?

MONA: I remember, yes.

HARTLEY: *(With increasing enthusiasm)* Well, now I see that you went beyond that, Mona. Somehow, through that murder, you managed to revert to the taproot of all drama everywhere!

MONA: All drama everywhere?

HARTLEY: These things are clouded in history, Mona, but scholars conjecture that in prehistoric times, many societies may have been matriarchal....

MONA: As with my grandmother, my mother, and me?

HARTLEY: Exactly! And every spring, these matriarchal societies would select a young man, and give him various honors and rewards—such as sleeping with the queen, for example....

MONA: Me? The queen? I'll take that as a compliment, Hartley.

HARTLEY: *(Moving into the aisles at this point)* As well
you should, Mona. But then, after he had slept with
the queen, they would get him drunk and sacrifice
him to the gods. Finally they would eat his body at a
communal feast, believing that his youthful energy and
power would be transferred to the tribe. In that way,
they hoped that the spring rains would fall, the corn
would grow, their enemies would be killed, et cetera
and so forth.

MONA: I see the parallels, yes....

HARTLEY: Those ancient events were a kind of primitive
theater, Mona. And they have continued, in one form
or another, for thousands of years. Greek drama,
for example, developed from these grim beginnings!

MONA: This is absolutely fascinating!

HARTLEY: And most subsequent drama, Mona, reflects
these ancient roots. Hamlet, Hedda Gabler, Willy
Loman are all sacrificial victims, taking on their
shoulders the sins of their particular times, and
are destroyed because of those sins. It's one way
of explaining tragedy.

MONA: Ah-hah.

HARTLEY: And of course, our celebrities and politicians
are our heroes today, playing out their dramas in the
vast arena of media publicity.

MONA: But are you saying we secretly want to murder,
castrate, and cannibalize our celebrities, Hartley?

HARTLEY: Exactly.

MONA: Wow.

HARTLEY: I'm saying they're the subject of today's
theater, and all theater is grounded in these primitive
rites. I'm saying that by inviting a lecturer to speak
on democracy, you made him into your own celebrity

and then fell back into that ancient groove. By murdering, castrating, and devouring him, Mona, you inadvertently revitalized your grandmother's dream, by reviving drama at its most basic level. *(He proudly pours himself another drink.)*

MONA: That's an extremely impressive analysis, Hartley.

HARTLEY: Remember, though, my field is drama, and this is anthropology. There may be a few loose ends.

MONA: No, no. It all makes a lot of sense.

HARTLEY: At least it explains why your lectureship program has been so successful. You've been riding on the communal guilt derived from that unfortunate murder.

MONA: That one murder, long ago?

HARTLEY: That one murder, long ago.

MONA: *(Carefully)* Don't the others count?

HARTLEY: There have been other murders?

MONA: Actually, yes.

HARTLEY: Occurring the same way?

MONA: Pretty much. Yes.

HARTLEY: But...why?

MONA: Our subscribers seemed to demand it.

HARTLEY: But who were the other victims?

MONA: Other guest lecturers.

(Pause)

HARTLEY: But surely the police...?

MONA: The police are active subscribers.

HARTLEY: But the graduate schools must have inquired about...

MONA: Graduate schools don't take attendance....

HARTLEY: But the families of these victims must have...

MONA: Family values are not what they used to be, Hartley.

(Long pause)

HARTLEY: Mona, I'm going to ask you something point blank.

MONA: Go ahead.

HARTLEY: Am I the next victim?

MONA: That's a rather bald way of putting it.

HARTLEY: I'm the next victim. Right?

MONA: *(To audience)* I *hate* this part. I loathe it.

HARTLEY: I'm the next *victim!* That's why you called this the danger seat! And that's why you're sitting in the driver's seat!

MONA: Oh, now...

HARTLEY: God, What a jerk I've been! What an idiot!

MONA: Now, now.

HARTLEY: No, but this is so typical of the academic mind! We think we know all the answers, but when it comes down to our own lives, we can't see our hand in front of our face! *(Slaps his forehead)* See better, Lear!

MONA: Now don't start punishing yourself!

HARTLEY: No, but it's obvious! The sacrificial lamb is me! —I! —Me! Shit! Aristotle says that every good play should have a recognition scene, and you've just taken me through a corker! I'm to be castrated, killed, and cannibalized right here, in front of this theater-starved multitude!

MONA: Not in *front*, Hartley. It never happens in front. It always happens offstage. Like the Greeks.

HARTLEY: Oh, yes? Well, I believe I know a little more about the Greeks than you do, Mona. And I can assure you that most Greek protagonists don't go easily to their own doom!

(He runs off left. We hear banging on a door.)

MONA: Um. That door is locked, Hartley.

HARTLEY: *(Coming back on)* What about the fire laws?

MONA: The fire chief has given us a waiver.

(HARTLEY starts off left.)

MONA: *Now* where are you going?

HARTLEY: I need to make a telephone call.

MONA: The phone is disconnected, Hartley. Too many guest lecturers misused it.

HARTLEY: Then I'll try the pay phone on the corner. See ya. *(He goes off left.)*

MONA: *(To audience)* This is the part I really hate. Every year, I hate it more and more!

(HARTLEY comes back on.)

HARTLEY: Fred wouldn't let me leave.

MONA: Oh, dear.

HARTLEY: He had Bruce pull a knife on me!

MONA: Oh, that's just a prop knife, Hartley, left over from my mother's production of *Deathtrap*.

HARTLEY: Oh, really. *(He goes upstage, gropes through the upstage drapes to find an opening; finally finds the split,*

confronts a blank brick wall with a sign saying "No Exit.")
It seems I'm a prisoner here.

MONA: Now stop this, Hartley! Be a man, for God's sake!

HARTLEY: I will—after I go to the men's room.
(He starts up the aisle.)

MONA: I'd stay away from that audience, Hartley.

HARTLEY: Why?

MONA: They can tear you apart. I've seen them do it.

(He clutches his groin, starts out a vom.)

MONA: There are men there.

(He looks at the other vom.)

MONA: There, too.

HARTLEY: *(Throwing himself at* PAT*)* Pat! Help me!

MONA: She can't, Hartley. She's on an entirely different contract.

*(*PAT *plays a sprightly song.)*

HARTLEY: Oh God, oh God, oh God.

MONA: Hartley.

HARTLEY: What?

MONA: I'm not happy with this.

HARTLEY: *You're* not happy!

MONA: I was hoping tonight might be different.

HARTLEY: This, from the high priestess of the temple of doom!

MONA: I'm tired of playing that part.

HARTLEY: Yeah, right.

MONA: I am! I'm tired of leading lecturers to slaughter. Ask anyone here. I expressed my reservations at the beginning of the evening. While you were having your cappuccino.

HARTLEY: Yeah, yeah.

MONA: What's more, I've grown fond of you personally. Particularly after we went to bed together.

HARTLEY: Oh, sure.

MONA: Seriously! I'd much prefer to see you walk out of this theater alive, and fully clothed, and sexually equipped. And I'll bet there are others here who feel the same.

HARTLEY: *(Glancing out)* You think?

MONA: There are people here who want to believe in you, Hartley.

HARTLEY: You make me feel like some fucking Tinkerbell.

MONA: Watch the language, please! We have teenagers present!

HARTLEY: But I'm dying here.

MONA: Then do something! You're the student of drama. I was hoping you'd come up with a dramatic solution.

HARTLEY: Let me think... *(He sits on the edge of the stage, thinks.)*

(PAT might play music from a popular game show.)

MONA: *(Watching him)* The clock is ticking away, Hartley.

HARTLEY: It's kind of hard to think under this pressure.... *(More thinking; more watching)*

MONA: *(Whispering)* Couldn't you speed things up?

HARTLEY: I'm trying, I'm trying....

MONA: *(Getting her purse)* I can see I have to help.

HARTLEY: How?

MONA: *(Producing a pistol)* Here. Use this.

HARTLEY: On myself?

MONA: On anyone who prevents your escape....
Get going.

HARTLEY: You got this for me?

MONA: This afternoon. After we went to bed together.
Now move!

HARTLEY: But what about you?

MONA: Me?

HARTLEY: Won't they take it out on you for betraying
your community?

MONA: I imagine they'll start a search for another
artistic director, yes.... But never mind! Go, go, go!

HARTLEY: O K.

*(He goes out left, pointing the gun with both hands, like
Dirty Harry. PAT plays a theme from some T V suspense
drama. MONA peers offstage.)*

MONA: Oh, no!

(HARTLEY comes back on.)

HARTLEY: I can't.

MONA: Why not?

HARTLEY: Because it's wrong, Mona.

. MONA: Leaving me?

HARTLEY: Leaving the stage this way. Shooting my way
out. Like some movie. Or television show. It's not true
drama.

MONA: Oh, Hartley.

HARTLEY: I'm serious. I couldn't live with myself afterwards. *(Hands her the gun)* Here. Save this for a rainy day.

MONA: But what else can you do?

HARTLEY: You asked for a dramatic solution. I've decided to produce one.

MONA: How?

HARTLEY: By putting my trust in the theater.

MONA: Trust?

HARTLEY: All good theater is built on trust, Mona—trust between actor and actor, actor and management, actor and audience. Without this trust, a play can't take place. With it, we can change the world.

MONA: Bravo! That's more like the man I slept with this afternoon! *(To audience)* Give him a hand, people!

(She encourages applause. PAT supports it with a musical theme from some heroic movie.)

MONA: Now explain what it means.

HARTLEY: First, this. *(Takes his note cards out, tosses them melodramatically into the air)* Goodbye to two and a half years of graduate school. I only went there because I couldn't make it as an actor.

MONA: Is that true?

HARTLEY: It is. Now I'm making my comeback on the living stage. *(Taking out a pen)* Lend me a piece of paper, Mona.

MONA: *(Indicating notecards)* Why don't you simply recycle one of those?

HARTLEY: Good point. *(Picks up a card, starts writing)* I want you to purchase the following things. You'll notice there are three items on this list. *(Hands it to her)*

MONA: Why three?

HARTLEY: Because there's a rule of three in the theater, Mona. I'd explain it further, but I think you'd learn more if you looked it up in the library.

MONA: *(Looking at the list)* But how will these things help?

HARTLEY: Trust me, Mona. Trust, remember?

MONA: *(Taking the list)* All right. A-shopping I will go. But why do I feel like singing?

HARTLEY: Because in Greek tragedy, when the pressure becomes too intense, the chorus bursts spontaneously into song.

MONA: Good. Then maybe Pat and I can finish our earlier number.

(PAT plays the intro.)

HARTLEY: Yes, but what do I do while you're singing?

(PAT stops playing.)

MONA: You could take a short break.

HARTLEY: I'd sure like to. The vodka in me wants out.

MONA: Then go, go, go. While I sing.

(PAT starts the intro again.)

HARTLEY: But how can I be sure I won't be ritually sacrificed once I'm in the wings?

(PAT stops playing.)

MONA: *(Handing him the gun again)* Good point. Take the gun. Just in case.

HARTLEY: Fair enough. *(Taking the gun, starting off)* I'm still nervous, though. I'm keeping my back to the wall at all times, even in the men's room!

(He goes. PAT *starts intro again.)*

MONA: *(Singing)* What's happening here?
What is the bidding?
Should I be showing my hand?

What's happening here?
Who am I kidding?
Is this thing going as planned?—

*(*FRED *comes on from the left.)*

FRED: I'll bet you sing that to all the boys.

MONA: Not with so much feeling, Fred.

FRED: You've fallen for this one, haven't you?

MONA: Maybe.

FRED: I'm a businessman, Mona. I have very little tolerance for ambiguity.

MONA: I happen to be quite fond of him, yes.

FRED: This is not some sentimental sitcom, Mona.

MONA: I determine the program around here, Fred.

FRED: There are times when the Board has to intervene.

MONA: I've decided to go in a different direction.

FRED: Oh, yes? We'll see.

*(*HARTLEY *comes back on.)*

HARTLEY: *(Returning the gun to* MONA*)* Thanks for this, Mona.

MONA: *(Putting it back in her purse)* You're most welcome.

HARTLEY: *(To* FRED*)* Hiya, Fred. *(Holding out his hand)* Good to see you again.

FRED: *(Walking away from him)* Save it for Sunday, kid.

MONA: Fred, for some reason, is in a very bad mood.

HARTLEY: So it would seem.

MONA: It's best if we just ignored him.

FRED: *(Wheeling on her)* Listen, you two-timing little tramp—

HARTLEY: *(Intervening)* Hey! Hey! Take it easy there, Fred.

*(*FRED *goes upstage, broods.)*

MONA: Thank you, Hartley.... Everything all right backstage?

HARTLEY: Yes, except...

MONA: Except what?

HARTLEY: On my way back, I happened to glance at the prop table.

MONA: *(To audience)* For our newer subscribers, the prop table is a table where people put props. *(To* HARTLEY*)* What did you see on the prop table, Hartley.

HARTLEY: I saw three things, Mona.

MONA: Three... Always three.

HARTLEY: I saw a braided silken cord....

MONA: And?

HARTLEY: A pair of extra-sharp pruning shears, from Smith and Hawken....

MONA: Yes. And?

HARTLEY: A used cookbook which appears to have been published in Papua, New Guinea.

MONA: I see.

HARTLEY: You can understand why I found them rather off-putting.

MONA: Did you put those props there, Fred?

FRED: It's a free country.

MONA: *(To* HARTLEY*)* Fred put those props there.

FRED: Yeah, well, maybe it's time to remind you folks where we're supposed to be going.

MONA: *(To* HARTLEY*)* Fred is obviously on the warpath. This may not be the best time for me to run those errands for you.

HARTLEY: Go ahead, Mona. Do it.

MONA: But once I'm gone, I can't guarantee your safety.

HARTLEY: *(Indicating the audience)* Then I'll count on the natural human decency of these good people.

MONA: Audiences can be fickle and unreliable, Hartley.

HARTLEY: Mona: I believe, I *have* to believe, that the American people have their good side, as well as an appalling instinct for violence. I'm counting on their better angels tonight. As long as I stay on this stage, basking in the warm light of their attention, I feel strangely safe.

MONA: God, Hartley! You've grown so much in the past half hour!

HARTLEY: That's because I have an action now. I know what to do.

MONA: Either way, you're wonderful.

FRED: Either way, you're history, kid.

MONA: Fred—

HARTLEY: I can handle him, Mona.

MONA: All right, then I'll go shopping. Even though I feel extremely nervous about what might happen in the next scene. *(She goes.)*

*(*HARTLEY *and* FRED *eye each other.)*

FRED: *(Indicating the danger seat)* Sit down, kid.

HARTLEY: *(Sitting)* All right.

FRED: Tell me about yourself.

HARTLEY: I already did, at the restaurant.

FRED: Tell me more.

HARTLEY: O K. I was born....

FRED: Cut to the chase, kid. How much do you contribute annually to the gross national product?

HARTLEY: Well, I hope someday to—

FRED: Do you consume?

HARTLEY: Do I...?

FRED: Buy things? Use things? Throw things away?

HARTLEY: Well, I...

FRED: You're in graduate school, aren't you?

HARTLEY: I was. I...

FRED: Old man pay the bills?

HARTLEY: No, as a matter of fact, I got a...

FRED: Government loan?

HARTLEY: No, a personal...

FRED: Ever thought of paying it off?

HARTLEY: Of course I'll....

FRED: Do you work?

HARTLEY: I do some undergraduate....

FRED: Call that teaching?

HARTLEY: I like to think....

FRED: How many hours a week do you so-called teach?

HARTLEY: Nine or ten, counting...

FRED: I work nine or ten hours a *day*!

HARTLEY: You don't have a thesis to....

FRED: My father worked eight days a *week*!

HARTLEY: Well, we live in different....

FRED: My grandfather worked fifty-two weeks a year and never took a vacation, except once, to Ocean City, New Jersey, when he rode the Bump-Mobiles.

HARTLEY: We're getting off the subject, Fred. I have a proposal to make.

FRED: You want to change something? *(To audience)* The graduate school grunt, who has never met a payroll in his life, wants to change the world.

HARTLEY: Oh, come on.

FRED: *(To audience)* Young Lochinvar out of the east wants to reinvent the wheel.

HARTLEY: Oh, now please....

FRED: My wife Bernice and I were among the first subscribers to this theater. We sit in the same seats every year.

HARTLEY: Congratulations.

FRED: When we need subscribers, Bernice gets on the phone. When we run a deficit, Bernice gets out the checkbook. When we need a benefit, Bernice makes the macaroni salad.

HARTLEY: Yes, well, I happen to think....

FRED: Do you realize that since our guest lecture series, the crime rate in this town has decreased thirty-nine percent?

HARTLEY: I don't think....

FRED: We have fourteen percent fewer divorces! Seventy-three percent of our youngsters now go to college, and sixty-two percent of these can read!

HARTLEY: I don't see....

FRED: Eighty-*six* percent of our senior citizens are continent! Forty-one percent of the time! Poverty has gone bye-bye. Homelessness is a no-no. Welfare is pee-pee, poo-poo, ca-ca. And listen to this, sonny boy: Our two-bit minor league ball club has made the interstate finals four out of the last six years. In 1997, we scored three consecutive runs on a full-court press, without even icing the puck!

HARTLEY: I didn't know that.

FRED: There's a lot you don't know, sonny. Why do you think these things happen? Because this community has had the guts to get together once a year in this theater, and do a little spring cleaning.

HARTLEY: Ah. You're talking about catharsis.

FRED: Come again?

HARTLEY: Catharsis. Aristotle called it catharsis.

FRED: *(To audience)* Mister Peepers comes up with a new word.

HARTLEY: Not a new word, sir. A very old word. Aristotle argued that good theater had a *cathartic*, or purging, effect on the *polis*, or city, cleansing it of its aggressive or selfish instincts and recementing its communal bonds.

FRED: Give it whatever cockamamie name you want, son, the thing works.

HARTLEY: May I have the floor now, please?

FRED: *(Walking away)* Go ahead.

HARTLEY: What you are defending, sir, are the communal benefits of good theater.

FRED: *(To audience)* Get out your shovels, gang. Here comes the shit.

HARTLEY: Give me a chance, Fred. I have no objections to your intentions, sir. I do have a problem with how you put them into practice. In your yearning for meaningful theater, you seem to have ventured into ritual murder.

FRED: Don't worry about it, kid. It's not your problem.

HARTLEY: It *becomes* my problem, sir, when I'm the intended victim.

FRED: *(To audience)* Everybody's a victim these days.

HARTLEY: I'd just as soon live out my life, Fred.

FRED: I. My. Me. When do you kids start thinking about the other guy? Love thy neighbor as thy*self*, my friend. Ever heard that one before? *(To audience)* My God, the public health is at stake here, and all he can come up with is the vertical pronoun: I, I, I. Aye, yi, yi.

HARTLEY: Fred, please. I want to make a deal with you.

FRED: *(To audience)* The professor wants to make deals now. The freeloader wants to shake hands with the real world. *(Grabbing* HARTLEY, *pulling him toward off left)* What say we give these good folks a break and work things out in the wings?

HARTLEY: *(Breaking away)* Oh, no you don't, Fred. I'm staying out here in the light.

FRED: Chicken.

HARTLEY: We can call each other names, Fred, or we can try to do business.

FRED: What's the deal, then?

HARTLEY: Suppose this community could have all the benefits of really exciting theater without actually killing anyone.

FRED: *(To audience)* Kid wants to have his cake without breaking an egg. *(To* HARTLEY*)* What's the hitch?

HARTLEY: The only hitch is, you have to sit and watch.

FRED: Watch? Like in T V?

HARTLEY: No. Not T V. In the theater, you have to watch *actively*. You have to collaborate. You have to *willingly* suspend your disbelief.

FRED: What if we don't feel like it?

HARTLEY: Then the theatrical transaction can't take place. But if you actively *bestow* on the theatrical event this special effort, then it makes me a better actor, and you a better person, and this community a better place to live.

FRED: Sounds fishy to me.

HARTLEY: Come on, Fred. Give it a try.

FRED: Naaaa. "Willingly suspend..." Doesn't fly, kid. *(Looks at watch)* Hey. It's getting late. The board meets in five minutes. *(Starts pulling* HARTLEY *again)*

HARTLEY: *(Desperately)* Tell the board I could save them money, Fred.

FRED: *(Stopping)* Money? Save money? How?

HARTLEY: With my proposal, think what you'd save on Prozac.

FRED: *(Angrily)* Who told you about the Prozac? That two-timing Mona?

HARTLEY: She did not, Fred. I just guessed. Considering what you've been up to, I figure the entire community must be popping at least one hundred and twenty milligrams of Prozac per person per day.

FRED: You're close.

HARTLEY: You could save that dough, Fred. And in the process, improve your sex life.

FRED: You don't know Bernice.

HARTLEY: No, I don't, Fred. But I'm hoping to meet her at the reception afterwards.

FRED: *(Thinking)* You want us to—what is it again? —willingly suspend our disbelief, eh?

HARTLEY: That's all I want, Fred.

FRED: But if things don't pan out, may we revert to ritual murder?

HARTLEY: Let's cross that bridge when we come to it, Fred. *(A noise off left)*

FRED: *(Looking off)* Mona's out there, waiting to come on. *(To* HARTLEY*)* Tell you what. I'll let the board vote on it. We're still a democracy, after all.

HARTLEY: Do that, Fred. And report back.

FRED: *(Pawing him, testing his flesh)* I have to say this, kid. Win or lose on the murder thing, you've shown some guts here tonight.

*(*MONA *comes on, carrying a shopping bag.)*

MONA: *(To* FRED*)* You boys solve the problems of the world?

FRED: It ain't that easy, Mona. *(He goes off.)*

MONA: I don't like the sound of that.

HARTLEY: I made him a proposal and he's bringing it up with the board.

MONA: That worries me. A *lot.*

HARTLEY: Maybe they'll listen to reason.

MONA: I don't know. I just heard several of them muttering in the wings. They're blaming you for everything that's wrong with contemporary America.

HARTLEY: See? They're heaping the sins of the community on my head so they'll have an excuse to kill me.

MONA: Anyway, I got what you wanted.

HARTLEY: *(Taking the shopping bag)* Thank you, Mona. I appreciate that.

MONA: I keep wanting to share with our subscribers what's there. *(To audience)* A towel. A play by Shakespeare. A—

HARTLEY: Stop! You'd ruin the suspense.

(FRED comes back on.)

FRED: Bad news, kid. The board just voted against you.

MONA: Knew it.

HARTLEY: They didn't take long to decide.

FRED: We didn't have to. We felt we shouldn't tamper with a tradition. It's like messing around with Thanksgiving.

MONA: Knowing you, Fred, you made a lousy presentation.

FRED: Listen, you dumb broad—

HARTLEY: *(Coming between them)* Easy! Simmer down, you two!

(FRED *and* MONA *simmer down.*)

HARTLEY: I knew the board would be difficult. I'll have to appeal to them in person.

FRED: Suit yourself, kid.

MONA: Don't go out there, Hartley.

HARTLEY: Have to, Mona. I need to dramatize my point.

MONA: But what if it doesn't work? I know the Board. It's ruthless and cruel. It's composed of overpaid C E Os and conservative Catholics.

FRED: We'll remember that crack when you come up for salary review, Mona.

HARTLEY: Tell them I intend to appear in front of them, Fred.

FRED: Fine. We'll be in the greenroom. *(He goes.)*

MONA: The greenroom! Hear that, Hartley? That's the scene of the crime, if you remember my earlier narrative.

HARTLEY: I remember it well.

MONA: Then don't go! The board can't touch you if you stay on stage. Actor's Equity wouldn't allow it.

HARTLEY: Mona, if I remained here in this comforting space, other plays might retreat from the larger issues, and American theater dwindle into triviality. *(He starts off.)*

MONA: Hartley! Wait! *(He stops.)* I've...I've never said this before, to any of our guest lecturers—well, I've *said* it but never really meant it.... I'd like to initiate a serious affair with you.

HARTLEY: I feel the same way. *(To audience)* The theater does that to us.

(PAT *plays romantic music.*)

HARTLEY: It creates bonds which makes outside relationships pale by comparison.

MONA: Do you have an outside relationship?

HARTLEY: I did. She now seems like a character in another play.

MONA: So does Fred.

HARTLEY: You and *Fred* had a relationship?

(PAT *stops playing.*)

MONA: Every spring, whenever we started making plans for the upcoming guest lecture, we copulated strenuously.

HARTLEY: That's disgusting!

MONA: No, now wait. Bernice knew and understood. I hope you will, too.

HARTLEY: I'll try. The theater can be a wonderfully forgiving place for those who commit their lives to it.

(PAT *starts playing a slow, menacing tom-tom beat.*)

HARTLEY: Why is Pat playing that menacing beat?

MONA: It means the board is getting impatient.

HARTLEY: It's a cheap effect, borrowed from *The Emperor Jones*, by Eugene O'Neill. Cut it out, Pat.

MONA: She tried to, once. But our subscribers asked for it back.

HARTLEY: I'd better go. I can't, Mona. Every instinct tells me it's time for me to stride manfully offstage!

(PAT's *rhythm increases.*)

MONA: *(Looking off)* But look! Now I see a number of shadowy figures lurking by the light board. The moment you step offstage, they'll grab you and pull your pants down!

HARTLEY: *(Looking off)* I see those shadowy figures, too. But I have to think they're theater interns from some community college, here to learn more about contemporary American drama.

(He kisses her; PAT again underscores it with romantic music.)

HARTLEY: Now goodbye. *(He strides toward the wings and then stops suddenly.)*

MONA: Now what?

HARTLEY: I'm trying to think of an exit line.

MONA: What about "I love you, Mona"?

HARTLEY: No. I can do better than that. *(Thinks briefly)* This is a little lame, but it will have to do. *(To audience)* If worse comes to worse out there, I only regret that I have but two balls to give to the theater.

MONA: That's the bravest line yet from a guest lecturer!

HARTLEY: Thanks, Mona. Now give me my props.

(He takes the shopping bag and strides off manfully. MONA watches him go. PAT's drumbeat continues more softly but insistently.)

MONA: *(Peering off)* He's gone. Swallowed up in that dusty, cluttered world we call backstage. *(To audience)* Now what? How many women over the centuries have found themselves roaming around an empty space, bereft of decent dialogue?

(PAT suddenly stops the drum beat.)

MONA: Uh-oh. Silence. I can imagine the board settling into their seats as he makes his presentation. Oh, I feel so helpless. But what can I do? He'd never forgive me if I let the air go out of this scene. I suppose I could talk about what he had in that bag. We Americans love to discuss our purchases. But he asked me not to. I'm torn

between my loyalty to him, and my confidence as
a consumer.... Oh, theater, theater, what a tough
taskmaster you have turned out to be!

(A scream from offstage)

MONA: Oh, God! What was that?

*(HARTLEY staggers on, naked except for his tie, which is
knotted tightly around his neck. With one hand, he clutches
a bloody white towel to his groin. With the other, he holds
a paperback copy of* Antony and Cleopatra. *He falls onto
the floor.)*

MONA: Oh, merciful heavens!

HARTLEY: *(Gasping)* Read this! *(He shudders and dies,
holding out the paperback Shakespeare, his finger in a
particular page.)*

MONA: *(Listening to his heart)* He's dead! *(Takes the book)*
Shakespeare's *Antony and Cleopatra*, open at a particular
page. *(Reads)* Act Four, scene fifteen! There's a passage
underlined. *(To audience)* Now remember: This is a cold
reading: *(Reads)*
"The crown o'th'earth doth melt! My Lord!
O, withered is the garland of the war,
The soldier's pole is fall'n; young boys and girls
Are level now with men. The odds is gone,
And there is nothing left remarkable
Beneath the visiting moon."

HARTLEY: *(Sitting up)* That is probably the finest piece
of dramatic poetry in the English language.

MONA: Hartley!

HARTLEY: Notice the castration imagery: "The soldier's
pole has fallen.... Men level now with boys...." It fits the
situation perfectly.

MONA: *(To audience)* He's alive and lecturing!

HARTLEY: *(Getting up)* How about this tie? I see it as a metaphor for how we strangle ourselves with the conventions of middle-class life.

MONA: Stop, Hartley. Please. *(She tries to embrace him.)*

HARTLEY: Careful. Ketchup can be a bitch to wash out.

MONA: *(To audience)* Ketchup was item number three! *(She kisses him.)*

HARTLEY: Did you think I was really dead?

MONA: Of course!

HARTLEY: See? That means you were suspending your disbelief!

MONA: *(Proudly)* I was, wasn't I?

HARTLEY: Then my plan worked, at least on you.

(FRED comes on, carrying a bathrobe.)

FRED: All right, put this on, young fella. Bernice has a problem with nudity on stage.

MONA: Bernice has a problem. Period.

(MONA covers HARTLEY's butt with the Shakespeare. FRED helps him with the bathrobe.)

HARTLEY: No, Mona, Bernice has a point. As Mark Twain said, clothes make the man, and naked people have little influence on society.... But tell me, Fred: Were you and the board convinced by my demonstration?

FRED: We'll wait and see what the critics say.

MONA: Typical.

FRED: *(Looking at his watch)* Hey, look, it's late. I've got a power breakfast tomorrow morning.

MONA: *(Sadly)* And Hartley's got to catch an early plane.

HARTLEY: Cancel my reservation, Mona. I can't retreat to the barren wastes of academia. Tonight I've tasted blood!

FRED: Now I'm confused. I thought it was just ketchup.

HARTLEY: It was blood to me, Fred! I want to stay here and help bring drama to the community! *(To audience)* We'll do Chekov, and Shakespeare, and Wendy Wasserstein!

MONA: What about our personal situation?

HARTLEY: We'll enjoy a rich relationship based on our common interest in good theater.

MONA: Sounds fine to me.

FRED: You two make me want to reexamine my partnership with Bernice.

MONA: That means we can finish our song! Take it, Pat!

(PAT starts to play.)

FRED: *(To audience)* And afterwards, we'll all mosey on over to the Holiday Inn for our communal feast.

MONA: *(To audience)* Yes. And for those who are concerned about the menu, remember that thanks to our guest lecturer, the hors d'oeuvres this year will be strictly vegetarian!

(PAT plays the song)

HARTLEY, MONA & FRED: *(Singing)*
This afternoon,
I thought you were small game...
I've changed my tune,
It's a different ballgame...

What's happening here?
What's the prognosis?

MONA: Moonlight and roses...

FRED: And double our grosses...

HARTLEY: Let's hope by osmosis
That something seeps through...

ALL: So what's happening here will happen in other
towns too!

(Stage effects here, if anyone wants them)

END OF PLAY

www.ingramcontent.com/pod-product-compliance
Lightning Source LLC
Chambersburg PA
CBHW052209090426
42741CB00010B/2465